by

Barbara Getty and Inga Dubay

Continuing Education Press
Portland State University
Portland, Oregon
www.cep.pdx.edu

ITALIC HANDWRITING SERIES

BOOK A ▪ Basic Italic
14 mm body height

BOOK B ▪ Basic Italic
11 mm, 9 mm

BOOK C ▪ Basic Italic
9 mm, 6 mm   Introduction to Cursive Italic

BOOK D ▪ Cursive Italic
6 mm, 5 mm   including Basic Italic

BOOK E ▪ Cursive Italic
6 mm, 5 mm, 4 mm   including Basic Italic

BOOK F ▪ Cursive Italic
6 mm, 5 mm, 4 mm   including Basic Italic

BOOK G ▪ Cursive Italic
5 mm, 4 mm   including Basic Italic

INSTRUCTION MANUAL

THIRD EDITION

Copyright 1994 by Barbara M. Getty and Inga S. Dubay
ISBN 978-0-87678-096-1

SECOND EDITION
Copyright 1986 by Barbara M. Getty and Inga S. Dubay
REVISED EDITION
Copyright 1980 by Barbara M. Getty and Inga S. Dubay
FIRST EDITION
Copyright 1979 by Barbara M. Getty and Inga S. Dubay

All rights reserved.
This text may not be reproduced in whole
or in part without the express written
permission of the copyright holder.

14 13 12 11 10 09 08 07 06

17 16 15 14 13 12 11 10 9 8

Published and distributed by
CONTINUING EDUCATION PRESS
PORTLAND STATE UNIVERSITY/ School of Extended Studies
P.O. BOX 1394 ▪ PORTLAND, OREGON 97207

Printed in the United States of America

Printed with soy ink   on recycled paper

CONTENTS

iv	Introduction	26	Join 3 *ao*
v	Basic & Cursive Italic Alphabet	27	Review
vi	Reminders	28	Join 4 *ae*
viii	Assessment Pre-test/Post-test	29	Review
		30	Join 5 *on*
1	**PART 1 Basic Italic**	35	Review
2	Families 1 & 2 *i j l · k v w x z*	36	Join 6 *rn*
3	Families 3 & 4 *n h m r · u y*	37	Review
4	Families 5 & 6 *a d g q · b p*	38	Join 7 *sn*
5	Families 7 & 8 *o e c s · f t*	39	Review
6	Capitals	40	Join 8 *aa*
7	Review, Numerals	42	Review
8	Uses of Basic Italic	43	Lifts
		44	Size, Slope, Spacing
9	**PART 2 Cursive Italic**	45	Slope Guidelines, Timed Writing
10	Transition		
12	Overview of Joins	46	Cursive Capitals
16	Review, Cursive Capitals	53	Letter/Booklet
17	Join 1 *an*	54	Reading Looped Cursive
19	Review	55	5mm lines
20	Join 2 *au*	56	4mm lines
25	Review		

INTRODUCTION

This is the fifth of seven books in the *Italic Handwriting Series*. It is recommended for fourth grade. This book is designed to provide further practice with cursive capitals and lowercase joins. For the student new to italic handwriting, an introduction to basic italic lowercase and capitals is provided, as well as an overview of the cursive joins.

Writing practice includes vowel sounds, consonant sounds, phonograms, prefixes, suffixes, and other letter combinations. Sentence content includes the five kingdoms of life, DNA, animal groups, minerals, vegetation zones/biomes, our solar system, and galaxies. Cursive capital practice includes origins of our alphabet and cities of the world. Application form, letter/booklet format and envelope making are also presented (see INSTRUCTION MANUAL for lines and template).

TEACHER/STUDENT INSTRUCTIONS: Writing process/stroke information, directions, notes, reminders, options, and assessments are included in the margins. Further letter and join descriptions and assessment questions are found in the INSTRUCTION MANUAL.

ASSESSMENT: Assessment is the key to improvement. The self-assessment method used enables the student to monitor progress. STEP 1: the student is asked to LOOK at the writing and affirm what is the best. Questions are asked requiring a yes/no answer. 'Yes' is affirmation of a task accomplished. 'No' indicates work to be done. STEP 2: the student is asked to PLAN what needs to be improved and how to accomplish this. STEP 3: the student is asked to put the plan into PRACTICE. This *LOOK, PLAN, PRACTICE* format provides self-assessment skills applicable to all learning situations. Letter shape is the first focus. The next focus is on size, spacing, and slope.

Eventually the student has a checklist: letter shape, letter size, letter spacing, and letter slope. Use the *Slope Guidelines* to enable the student to find a personal slope choice. Speed is encouraged after letterforms and joins are learned. *Timed Writing* enables a gradual increase in the number of words written per minute while maintaining comfort and legibility. Repeat *Timed Writing* once a month. *Reading Looped Cursive* provides experience reading another writing style, while comparing legibility with italic handwriting.

CLASSROOM MANAGEMENT: Using direct instruction, present two pages a week, with follow-up practice on lined paper. Demonstrate the process/stroke sequence for letters and joins. This instruction, together with opportunities for integrating handwriting into other areas of curriculum, can provide 20 to 30 minutes, 3 to 4 times a week. From day one, have DESK STRIPS and WALL CHART in place. For extra practice use BLACKLINE MASTERS. Have lined paper available that matches the 5mm and 4mm lines used in this book (see *Reminders*). Lines at the back of this book and in the INSTRUCTION MANUAL may be duplicated. Use thin paper for tracing over models in the book. Provide the opportunity for each student to select a page of his/her best handwriting to include in the student's portfolio.

As a teacher, your interest and enthusiasm are instrumental in attaining the goal of legible and neat handwriting. Pleasure in good handwriting is caught, not taught. The enjoyment of good handwriting is shared by both the writer and the reader. Handwriting is a lifelong skill. Good handwriting is a lifelong joy!

N.B. The information sources for the writing practice are *The New Reading Teacher's Book of Lists; Life Nature Library; Rand McNally World Atlas; Biology: A guide to the Natural World*, David Krogh; *Biology: Understanding Life*, Sandra Alters; and the Oregon Museum of Science & Industry. Source for origins of the alphabet is *Ancient Writing & Its Influence*, Berthold Ullman.

BASIC & CURSIVE ITALIC ALPHABET

BASIC ITALIC

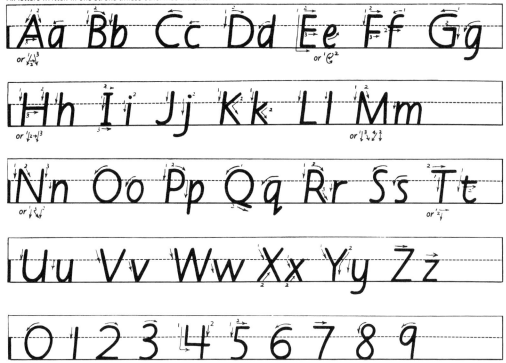

CURSIVE ITALIC

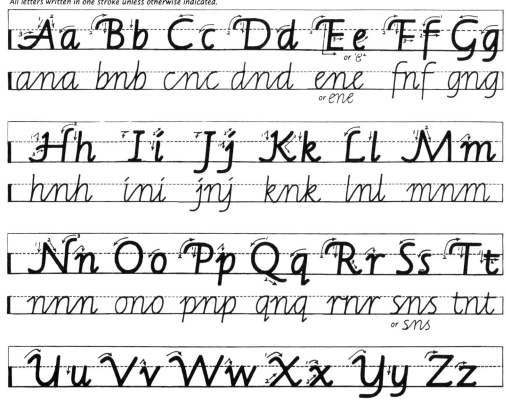

© 1994 Getty/Dubay

REMINDERS

PENCIL HOLD

Use a soft lead pencil (#1 or #2) with an eraser. Hold the pencil with the thumb and index finger, resting on the middle finger. The upper part of the pencil rests near the large knuckle.

REGULAR HOLD

Hold the pencil firmly and lightly. AVOID pinching. To relax your hand, tap the index finger on the pencil three times.

Problem grips such as the 'thumb wrap' (thumb doesn't touch pencil) and the 'death grip' (very tight pencil hold) make it difficult to use the hand's small muscles. To relieve these problems, try this alternative pencil hold.

ALTERNATIVE HOLD

Place the pencil between the index finger and the middle finger. The pencil rests between the index and middle fingers by the large knuckles. Hold the pencil in the regular way at the tips of the fingers.

PAPER POSITION

LEFT HANDED
If you are left-handed and write with the wrist below the line of writing, turn the paper clockwise so it is slanted to the right as illustrated. If you are left-handed and write with a "hook" with the wrist above the line of writing, turn the paper counter clockwise so it is slanted to the left as illustrated. (Similar to the right-handed position)

RIGHT-HANDED
If you are right-handed turn the paper counter-clockwise so it is slanted to the left as illustrated.

POSTURE

Rest your feet flat on the floor and keep your back comfortably straight without slumping. Rest your forearms on the desk. Hold the workbook or paper with your non-writing hand so that the writing area is centered in front of you.

LINED PAPER CHOICES:

The following choices for lined paper may be used when instructions say use lined paper for practice.

1. Lines 5mm body height on page 55 may be duplicated. These lines can also be used as guidelines under a sheet of unlined paper. Fasten with paper clips.

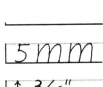

2. Lines 4 mm body height on page 56 may be duplicated. These lines can also be used as a line guide under a sheet of unlined paper.

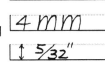

3. Some school paper has a solid baseline and a dotted waistline. Use paper with a body height of 6mm ($^1/_4$") or 5mm ($^3/_{16}$").

4. Some school paper has only baselines. Use paper with lines 12mm ($^1/_2$") or 10mm ($^3/_8$") apart.

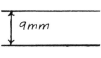

5. Use wide-ruled notebook paper with a space of about 9 mm ($^3/_8$") between lines. Create your own waistline by lining up two sheets of notebook paper and shifting one down half a space. The faint line showing through will serve as a waistline. Fasten with paper clips.

VOCABULARY

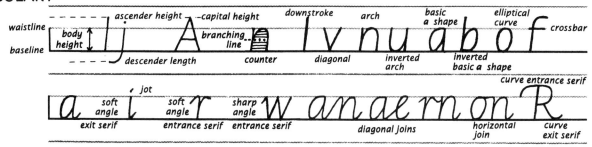

STROKES

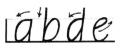

Basic italic letters all start at the top and go down or over (horizontal), except **d** and **e**, (**d** starts at the waistline and **e** starts at the center of the body height). Follow the direction of the arrow. Letters are written in one stroke unless otherwise indicated. Trace the dotted line model, then copy model in space provided. If needed, trace solid line model.

LETTER DIMENSIONS

SHAPE
Basic italic lowercase letters are divided into eight families according to shape. Basic italic capitals are divided into three width groups. Cursive italic lowercase joins are divided into eight join groups.

SIZE
Letters are written with a consistent body height. Capitals, ascenders and descenders are written one and a half times the body height.

SLOPE
The models are written with a 5° letter slope. A consistent slope is an important part of good handwriting. For individual slope choices see *Slope Guidelines*, page 45.

SPACING
Letters are written close together within words. Joins are natural spacers in cursive italic; when lifts occur, keep letters close together. Spacing between words is the width of an **n** in basic and cursive italic.

SPEED
Write at a comfortable rate of speed. Though speed is not a primary concern at this level, students may use the *Timed Writing*, page 45.

GOAL
To write legible, neat handwriting.

IMPROVEMENT
Assessment is the key to improving your handwriting. Follow this improvement method as you learn basic and cursive italic handwriting.

 LOOK at your writing. Circle your best letter or join. Answer question about strokes, shape, size, spacing, or slope.

 PLAN how to make your writing look more like the model. Pick the letter or join that needs work. Compare with the model.

 PRACTICE the letter or join that needs work. Write on the lines provided and on lined paper.

 Give yourself a star at the top of the page when you see you have made an improvement.

NOTE: See INSTRUCTION MANUAL, Assessment, pp. 54-68.

© 1994 Getty/Dubay

Pre-test/ Post-test

INFORMAL ASSESSMENT OF STUDENT PROGRESS

The main purpose of handwriting instruction is to promote legibility so that we can communicate with others and ourselves.

PRE-TEST Before you begin this book, write the following sentence in your everyday handwriting. Also write your name, address and today's date.

A quick brown fox jumps over the lazy dog.

POST-TEST After you have completed this workbook, write the following sentence in cursive italic. Also write your name, address and today's date in cursive italic.

A quick brown fox jumps over the lazy dog.

ASSESSMENT
- SHAPE: Each letter is similar to the models in the workbook.
- SIZE: Similar letters are the same height (for example: aec, dhk, gpy). Capital letters and lowercase letters with ascenders are the same height.
- SLOPE: Letters have a consistent letter slope (between 5° – 15°).
- SPACING: Letters within words are closely spaced. Spaces between words are the width of **n**.
- SPEED: Words are written fluently at a comfortable speed.

PART I
BASIC ITALIC

LOWERCASE: 8 families

Family 1. straight line downstroke - i j l
Family 2. diagonal line - k v w x z
Family 3. arch - n h m r
Family 4. inverted arch - u y
Family 5. basic *a* shape - a d g q
Family 6. inverted basic *a* shape - b p
Family 7. elliptical curve - o e c s
Family 8. crossbar - f t

Improvement: shape, size

CAPITALS: 3 width groups

1. wide width - C G O Q D M W
2. medium width - T H A N K U V X Y Z
3. narrow width - E F L B P R S J I

Improvement: shape, size

LOWERCASE AND CAPITALS

Improvement: size, slope, spacing

NUMERALS

abcdefghijklmnopqrstuvwxyz

BASIC ITALIC LOWERCASE

NOTE: Letters in each family are alike in some way. Can you tell how letters in each family are alike?

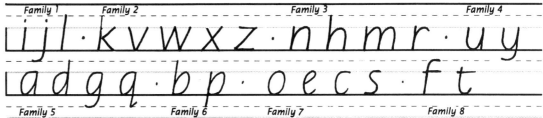

FAMILY 1: STRAIGHT LINE DOWNSTROKE

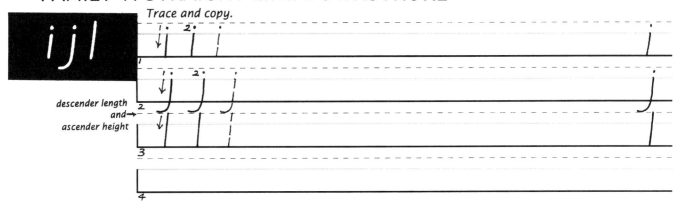

Trace and copy.

descender length and ascender height

✏ Circle your best **i, j,** and **l**.

FAMILY 2: DIAGONAL LINE

kvwxz

HINT: The corner of a sheet of paper fits here. This is a right angle.

baseline

✏ Circle your best **k, v, w, x,** and **z**.

NOTE: For assessment questions see INSTRUCTION MANUAL.

© 1994 Getty/Dubay

Basic Italic Lowercase
FAMILY 3: ARCH

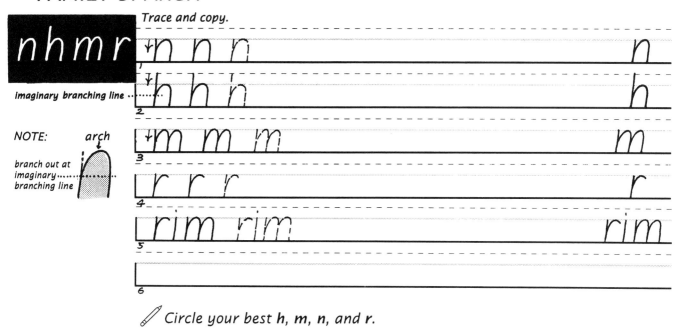

Trace and copy.

imaginary branching line

NOTE: arch
branch out at imaginary branching line

✏️ Circle your best **h, m, n,** and **r**.

FAMILY 4: INVERTED ARCH (UPSIDE-DOWN ARCH)

branching line

NOTE:
upside down arch
branch in at imaginary branching line

[1] LOOK at your writing. Pick your best letters.

[2] Pick the letters that need work. Compare them with the models. PLAN how to make them look more like the models.

[3] PRACTICE

✏️ Circle your best **u** and **y**.

HINT:
Turn **n** upside down to see **u**.

3 © 1994 Getty/Dubay

Basic Italic Lowercase
FAMILY 5: BASIC a SHAPE

adgq

branch in at imaginary branching line

Trace and copy.

a a a   a
d d d   d
g g g   g
q q q   q
and and   and
aqua aqua   aqua

NOTE: branch in at imaginary branching line — *a shape*

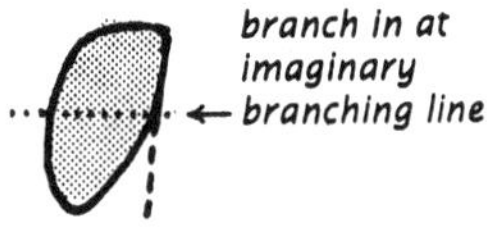

HINT: flat head — soft angle (chin) curve

✏️ Circle your best **a, d, g,** and **q**.

FAMILY 6: INVERTED BASIC a SHAPE (UPSIDE-DOWN BASIC a SHAPE)

b p

imaginary branching line

b b b   b
p p p   p
bump   bump

NOTE: branch out at imaginary branching line — *upside-down a shape*

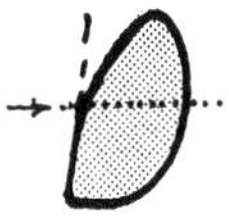

✏️ Circle your best **b** and **p**.

HINTS:
Turn d upside down to see p.

Turn q upside down to see b.

© 1994 Getty/Dubay

Basic Italic Lowercase

FAMILY 7: ELLIPTICAL CURVE

o e c s

Trace and copy.

o o o   o
e e e   e
c c c   c
s s s   s

imaginary branching line ··· e

NOTE: *e center of body height*

oceans oceans

Notice this reads the same right side up as it does upside down. **pod**

✏ Circle your best **o**, **e**, **c**, and **s**.

FAMILY 8: CROSSBAR

f t

f f f   f
t t t   t
fast fast   fast
ft ft ft ft   ft
lift lift   lift

NOTE: *The crossbar joins f and t.* **ft**

Ascender of t is shorter than the ascender of f. **ft**

✏ Circle your best **f** and **t**.

[1] LOOK at your writing.

[2] PLAN which letters need work. How will you make them look more like the models?

[3] PRACTICE the letters that need more work.

© 1994 Getty/Dubay

BASIC ITALIC CAPITALS: WIDE, MEDIUM AND NARROW

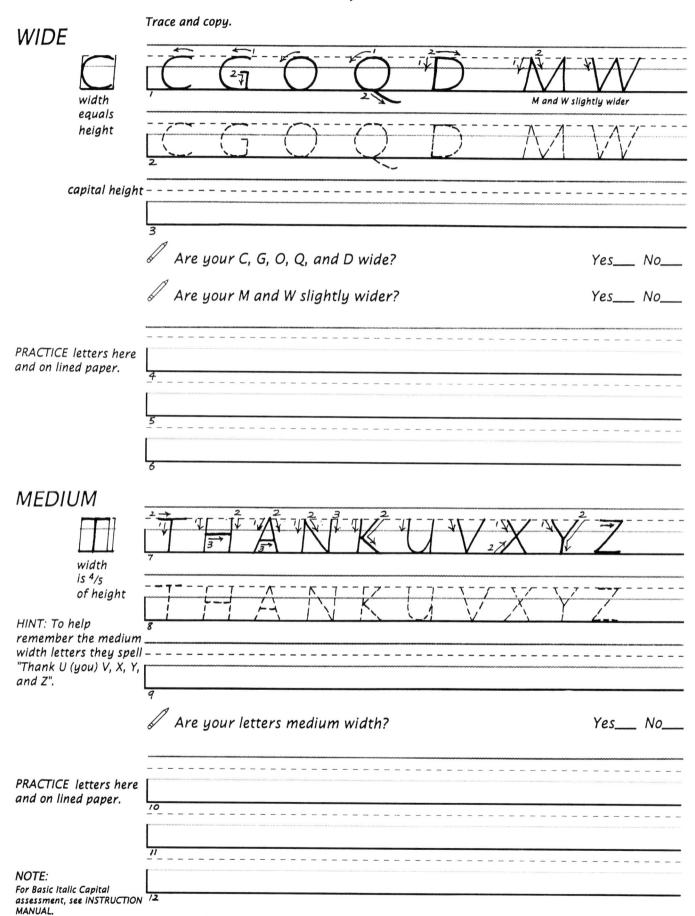

Basic Italic

NARROW

width is ½ of height

Trace and copy.

E F L B P R S J I

E F L B P R S J I

✏ Are your letters narrow width?   Yes___ No___

PRACTICE letters here and on lined paper.

REVIEW: BASIC ITALIC CAPITALS AND LOWERCASE

Aa Bb Cc Dd Ee Ff Gg

A

Hh Ii Jj Kk Ll Mm Nn

Oo Pp Qq Rr Ss Tt Uu

Vv Ww Xx Yy & Zz

🧊 1
LOOK at your writing. Pick your best letters.

🧊 2
Pick the letters that need work. Compare them with the models. PLAN how to make them look more like the models.

🧊 3
Place lined paper over the models and trace. PRACTICE on lined paper.

NUMERALS: The size of numerals is one body height.

0 1 2 3 4 4 5 5 6 7 8 9 10 11 12

O

© 1994 Getty/Dubay

Basic Italic

PANGRAM: A sentence containing all the letters in the alphabet. Trace and copy.

Body height is 5mm (previous body height was 6mm).

A quick brown fox jumps over the lazy dog. A

SLOPE: Straight line downstrokes are parallel to 5° slope.

See Slope Guidelines on page 45.

PRACTICE writing with an even slope.

SPACING: There are three widths of spacing letters in words:

1. Wide space between straight line downstrokes.

2. Medium space between straight line and curve.

3. Narrow space between two curves at the center. Narrow space between diagonal and downstroke at the waistline.

hill
home
pod
wavy

PRACTICE writing using even letter spacing.

PRACTICE writing using the width of an n between words.

Leave the width of n between words.

USING BASIC ITALIC

Basic italic, sometimes called "printing", is useful for many writing purposes, such as messages, posters, maps, announcements, recipes, and for filling out application forms. When a form says "Please print", use basic italic.

Complete this application form using your best basic italic handwriting.

APPLICATION FORM   Please print

Name: _____
         Last   First   Middle

Address: _____
              Street

         _____
              City   State   Zip Code

School: _____   Age: _____

© 1994 Getty/Dubay

PART 2

CURSIVE ITALIC

TRANSITION TO CURSIVE ITALIC

Changes in letter shape - f and k
Jot for i and j
Serifs: soft angle exit serifs - a d h i k l u n m z
   soft angle entrance serifs - r n m x z
   sharp angle entrance serifs - j p v w

Improvement: shape

CURSIVE ITALIC LOWERCASE: 8 JOINS

Join 1. diagonal - an
Join 2. diagonal swing up - au
Join 3. diagonal start back - ao
Join 4. diagonal into e - ae
Join 5. horizontal - on
Join 6. diagonal out of r - ru
Join 7. horizontal to diagonal - sn
Join 8. diagonal to horizontal - aa
Lifts - lift before f and z; lift after g j q y
Review

Vowel sounds, consonant sounds, phonograms, prefixes, suffixes, letter and envelope writing

Improvement: shape, size, spacing, slope

CURSIVE CAPITALS

Origins: Egyptian, Phoenician, Greek, Roman
Basic Italic and Cursive Italic
Writing practice using cities of the world

Improvement: shape, size, slope

READING LOOPED CURSIVE

Comparison of cursive italic handwriting with looped cursive handwriting

SLOPE, SPEED

Slope Guidelines
Timed Writing

LINES

5mm, 4mm

abcdefghijklmnopqrstuvwxyz

TRANSITION TO CURSIVE ITALIC

CHANGES: LETTER SHAPE; JOT ADDED Trace and copy.

f adds a descender   *k becomes a one-stroke letter*

f·f f   k·k k

i and j use a jot (A dot may be used instead of a jot.)

i·i i   j·j j

SERIFS: Serifs are lines added to letters.
There are exit serifs and entrance serifs.

Serifs are like hands reaching out to join letters.

EXIT SERIF: End with a soft angle at the baseline
into a short diagonal. (n, m, and x also have entrance serifs.)

← diagonal
↑ soft angle

a·a a   d·d d
h·h h   i·i i

AVOID a hook

k·k k   l·l l

AVOID a scoop

m·m m   n·n n
u·u u   x·x x

1. LOOK at your writing. Pick your best letters. Answer the question.
   ✏ Circle some of your best exit serifs.
   ✏ Are your letters ending with a soft angle exit serif?

2. Pick the letters that need work. Compare them with the models. PLAN how to make them look more like the models.

3. PRACTICE here the letters that need work.

10   © 1994 Getty/Dubay

Transition from Basic Italic to Cursive Italic

ENTRANCE SERIFS:

There are two kinds of entrance serifs—soft angle entrance serifs and sharp angle entrance serifs.

SOFT ANGLE
ENTRANCE SERIF: Begin with a short diagonal line to a soft angle. (m, n, and x have exit serifs also)

m·m·m   n·n·n

r·r·r   x·x·x

✏ Circle your best soft angle entrance serif.

SHARP ANGLE
ENTRANCE SERIF: Begin with a short diagonal line to a sharp angle.

j·j·j   p·p·p

v·v·v   w·w·w

✏ Circle your best sharp angle entrance serif.

PRACTICE the letters that need more work.

AVOID a scoop

CURSIVE Z: Add short entrance and exit serifs to z.   *z·z·z*

✏ Circle your best z.

REVIEW: CURSIVE ITALIC LOWERCASE LETTERS

No change: b, c, e, g, o, q, s, t, and y.

a b c d e f g h i j k l m

① Trace and copy. LOOK at your writing.   *a*

② PLAN which letters need work.   *n o p q r s t u v w x y z*

③ PRACTICE those letters on lined paper.   *n*

11

© 1994 Getty/Dubay

CURSIVE ITALIC LOWERCASE: 8 JOINS

JOIN 1: DIAGONAL Join with a straight diagonal line.

an an an an an an

Trace and copy.

Serifs are like hands reaching out to join letters.

in in in in in

en en en en

un un un un un

em er ex

em

im ir ix

im

um um ur ux

✏️ Are you using a straight diagonal line for the join? Yes___ No___

1. LOOK at your writing. Answer the question.
2. PLAN which joins need work. How will you make them look more like the models?
3. PRACTICE the joins that need more work.

JOIN 2: DIAGONAL SWING UP Join with a straight diagonal line.

au au au au au au

Serifs reach out to join letters.

ay ai at

ay ai at

12

© 1994 Getty/DUBAY

Cursive Italic Lowercase

Trace and copy.   aj aj   ap ap
               an an   aw aw

Serifs reach out to join letters with ascenders.

               al al al al   al

imaginary branching line   ah   ak   ab
               ah   ak   ab
               el el   eh eh   eb eb   ek ek
               ei

✏ Are you joining at the imaginary branching line?   Yes___ No___

PRACTICE the joins
that need more work. |_____

JOIN 3: DIAGONAL START BACK Join with a straight diagonal line.

ao   ao ao ao ao   ao
         as as   as

Serifs reach up to the waistline.

         eo eo   io io   uo uo
         eo
NOTE: For another
join into s, see Join 8.   es es   is is   us us
         es

✏ Are you joining into **o** and **s** with a straight diagonal line?   Yes___ No___

PRACTICE the joins
that need more work. |_____

© 1994 Getty/Dubay

Cursive Italic Lowercase

JOIN 4: DIAGONAL INTO e Join with a diagonal line.

ae   ae ae ae ae   ae

Trace and copy.

Join out of e into all letters (except f and z).

ee ee   ie ie   ue ue

ee

✏️ Are you joining into e at the branching line?   Yes___ No___

PRACTICE the joins that need more work.

JOIN 5: HORIZONTAL Join with a horizontal line at the waistline.

ou   ou ou ou ou   ou

Reach out along the waistline.

on on   oo oo   oa oa

on

tu tu tu   Reach out from the crossbar.

fo fo   fa fa

vi wi vi wi   xi xi

vi wi   xi

□1 LOOK at your writing. Answer the question.

□2 PLAN which joins need more work.

□3 PRACTICE the joins that need more work.

✏️ Are you joining with a horizontal join out of o, t, f, v, and x? Yes___ No___

14   © 1994 Getty/DUBAY

Cursive Italic Lowercase

JOIN 6: DIAGONAL OUT OF r *Join with a short diagonal line.*

ru

Trace and copy.

ru ru ru ru   ru

It's just a short reach out of r.

rn rn   ro ro   ra ra   re re

✎ Are you joining out of r with a short diagonal line?   Yes___ No___

PRACTICE the joins that need work.

JOIN 7: HORIZONTAL TO DIAGONAL *Join with a horizontal line blending into a diagonal line.*

sn

sn sn sn sn   sn

su su   so so   bo po

se   be   pe

Follow back out of s, b, and p.

✎ Are you joining out of b, p, and s with a diagonal line?   Yes___ No___

PRACTICE the joins that need work.

JOIN 8: DIAGONAL TO HORIZONTAL *Join with a diagonal line blending into a horizontal line.*

aa

aa aa aa aa   aa

ac ad ag aq as

ac

Reach out to join into a, c, d, g, q, and s.

✎ Are you joining with a diagonal into the horizontal top of a, c, d, g, q, and s?
    Yes___ No___

PRACTICE the joins that need more work.

Cursive Italic

REVIEW: CURSIVE ITALIC LOWERCASE JOINS

JOIN 1 an · an   JOIN 2 all · all

JOIN 3 ao · ao   JOIN 4 ae · ae

JOIN 5 on · on   JOIN 6 ru · ru

JOIN 7 sn · sn   JOIN 8 aa · aa

Body height is 5mm (previous body height was 6mm).

The letter **n** is used to show how to join into and out of letters.

CURSIVE ITALIC CAPITALS AND LOWERCASE

Aana Bbnb Ccnc Ddnd

Eene Ffnf Ggng Hhnh

Iini Jjnj Kknk Llnl

Mmnm Nnnn Oono Ppnp

Qqnq Rrnr Ssns or sns Ttnt

Uunu Vvnv Wwnw Xxnx

Yyny Zznz

A quick brown fox jumps over the lazy dog.

LOOK at your writing. Pick your best letters.

Pick the letters that need work. Compare them with the models. PLAN how to make them look more like the models.

PRACTICE the letters that need more work.

For Cursive Italic Capitals and Lowercase assessment see INSTRUCTION MANUAL pp. 65-66.

16   © 1994 Getty/Dubay

CURSIVE ITALIC LOWERCASE
JOIN 1: DIAGONAL

*Join 1 is a straight diagonal line from the baseline to the waistline into **n**, **m**, **r**, and **x**.*

a̋ an
diagonal
to soft angle

an an en in kn mn un
Trace & copy. an

Double n
Silent n

nn running n autumn
nn

PREFIX: en-
SUFFIX: -en

en- encourage -en taken
en

CONSONANT SOUND:
KN: N sound
PREFIX: un-

kn know un- unusual
kn

PREFIX: in-

im- include · insect
im

lacewing

✏ Circle your best diagonal join into **n**.

a̋ am
diagonal
to soft angle

am am em im mm um
am

PREFIX: im-
Double m

im- impatient mm mammal
im

✏ Circle your best diagonal join into **m**.

PRACTICE here and
on lined paper.

17 © 1994 Getty/Dubay

Cursive Italic Lowercase - Join 1

ar ar
diagonal
to soft angle

ar ar cr dr er ir kr ur
Trace & copy. ar

VOWEL SOUNDS:
AR: AIR sound
AR: AR sound

ar care   ar larva
ar

ER: R sound
IR: R sound

er mineral   ir girl
er

UR: R sound
PHONOGRAM: * -ur

ur murmur   -ur fur
ur

CONSONANT SOUNDS:
CR: CR blend
DR: DR blend
SUFFIX: -er

cr crab   dr draw   -er smaller
cr

Metamorphosis:
egg to larva (caterpillar)
to chrysalis (pupa)
to adult butterfly

egg
larva
chrysalis
butterfly

✏️ Circle your best diagonal join into **r**.

All insects have a three-part
body: head, thorax and abdomen.
A

NOTE:
AVOID a wavy line
in

✏️ Are you AVOIDING a wavy line?   Yes___   No___

head
thorax
abdomen

wingless wasp

All insects have six legs (thorax area). Some insects have wings; others are wingless.

PRACTICE the joins
that need more work.

* PHONOGRAM: A
phonogram is a vowel
sound plus a
consonant sound. It is
often less than a
syllable. It needs an
initial consonant or
blend to make it a
word.

© 1994 Getty/Dubay

Cursive Italic Lowercase - Join 1

a͗ ax͂
diagonal
to soft angle

ax ax ex ix ux x x
Trace and copy. ax

PREFIX: ex-
PHONOGRAM: -ax

ex exist explore -ax wax
ex

CONSONANT SOUND:
X: KS sound

x mix next lynx
x

✏ Circle your best diagonal join into **x**.

REVIEW: JOIN 1

JOIN 1 joins are underlined.

NOTE: Write t and e close together. AVOID a gap between t and e.

The five kingdoms of life are animals, bacteria, fungi, plants, and protists.
T

[1] LOOK at your writing. Pick your best join. Answer the question.

✏ Circle one of your best diagonal joins.

[2] Pick the joins that need work. Compare them with the models. PLAN how to make the joins look more like the models.

✏ Are you using a straight line for your diagonal join? Yes___ No___

[3] PRACTICE those joins here and on lined paper.

Cursive Italic Lowercase

JOIN 2: DIAGONAL SWING UP

Join 2 is a straight diagonal line from the baseline to the branching line, then swing up to the waistline or ascender height into **b, h, i, j, k, l, p, t, u, v, w,** and **y.**

a, au
diagonal swing up

Trace & copy.   au   au cu du eu hu iu ku lu
au

Double u

Letters join at the branching line.   mu nu zu · uu vacuum

imaginary branching line   mu

VOWEL SOUND:
AU: broad O

au caution dinosaur
au

Tyrannosaurus Rex

✏ Circle one of your best joins into **u**.

a, ay
diagonal swing up

ay   ay cy dy ey iy ky ly my
ay

SUFFIX: -ly

ny uy -ly slowly neatly
ny

VOWEL SOUND:
AY: long A
SUFFIX: -cy

ay clay layer -cy accuracy
ay

SUFFIX: -y

-y cloudy rainy sunny
y

✏ Circle one of your best joins into **y**.

PRACTICE the joins that need more work.

Cursive Italic Lowercase - Join 2

a ↗ ai
diagonal
swing up

ai | ai ci di ei hi ki li mi ni
Trace & copy. ai

Double i
PHONOGRAM: -ain

ui zi · ii skiing -ain brain
ui

VOWEL SOUND:
AI: long A
PHONOGRAM: -air

ai aid rain -air hair pair
ai

✏ Circle your best join into **i**.

a ↗ aj
a ↗ ap
diagonal
swing up
PHONOGRAMS:
-ap, -amp, -ump.

aj ap | aj ap ej ep ip lp mp up
aj

-ap map -amp lamp -ump lump
ap

✏ Circle your best join into **p** and **j**.

Join 2 joins are underlined.

DNA is in all living things.

(DNA- deoxyribonucleic acid)

DNA contains the blueprint for life

OPTION: You may dot **i** and **j**.

21   © 1994 Getty/DuBay

Cursive Italic Lowercase - Join 2

a → at — diagonal swing up

at | at ct et it lt nt ut
Trace & copy. | at

PHONOGRAMS: -at, -int

-at cat mat that -int print
at

REMINDER: t has a short ascender.

SUFFIX: -ant

Double t
-ant assistant tt spotted
ant

NOTE: DOUBLE T — long crossbar
U tt — large U shape

✏ Does your t have a short ascender? Yes___ No___

a → al — diagonal swing up

silent l
al | al cl el il ll ul · l half
at

VOWEL SOUND: AL: broad O
PHONOGRAM: -all

al always salt -all small
al

PHONOGRAMS: -ell, -ill, -ull

-ell shell -ill hill -ull gull
ell

CONSONANT SOUND: CL: CL blend
PHONOGRAM: -ilt

cl clear include -ilt quilt
cl

SUFFIXES: -al, -ily

-al natural -ily happily
al

NOTE: imaginary branching line
Join into l at the branching line.

at

✏ Circle one of your best joins into l.

AVOID
al
scoop and loop

© 1994 Getty/Dubay

Cursive Italic Lowercase - Join 2

a↗ a′h
diagonal swing up

| **ah** | ah ch eh ih uh h honest |

Trace & copy. ah

CONSONANT SOUND:
CH: digraph

ch lunch chipmunk
ch

✏️ Circle your best join into **h**.

a↗ a′b
diagonal swing up

| **ab** | ab eb ib lb mb ub b thumb |

PHONOGRAMS: -ab, -ib, -ub, -umb

-ab crab -ib rib -ub cub -umb

✏️ Circle your best join into **b**.

a↗ a′k
diagonal swing up

| **ak** | ak ck ek ik lk nk uk |

ak

Silent k
PHONOGRAM: -ank

k knowledge -ank sank clank
k

PHONOGRAMS: -ink, -unk, -alk, -ick

-ink sink clink -unk sunk clunk
ink

-alk talk -ick pick flicker
alk

✏️ Circle your best join into **k**.

PRACTICE here and on lined paper.

© 1994 Getty/Dubay

Cursive Italic Lowercase - Join 2

a↗ av
a↗ aw
diagonal swing up

VOWEL SOUND:
AW: broad O
PHONOGRAM: -ew

OPTION: v and w may be written with either a sharp angle or a soft angle at the baseline.

Trace & copy.

av aw   av aw ev ew iv iw
                sharp angle v   sharp angle w
av
aw awe claw -ew few knew
aw
av aw ev ew iv iw claw
soft angle v   soft angle w
av

✏ Circle your best join into **v** and **w**.

Quagga (South Africa) extinct since the 19th century.

5° SLOPE

During the last fifty years many species of mammals have vanished. Today, several hun-dred are threatened with extinction.

NOTE: HYPHEN
Use a short dash when separating syllables of a word on different lines.

PRACTICE writing with an even slope.

See Slope Guidelines on page 45.

✏ Are you using a 5° slope?   Yes___ No___

OPTION: You may use Join 2 to join into **n, m, r,** and **x**.

Join at the imaginary branching line.

an en in un · am em im um
an

imaginary branching line ar er ir ur · ax ex ix ux
ar

© 1994 Getty/Dubay

Cursive Italic Lowercase
REVIEW: JOIN 2

The major animal groups are:

JOIN 2 joins are underlined.

amphibians: 3,000 species

birds: 8,600 species

fishes: 20,000 species

insects: 800,000 species and

other invertebrates: 350,000 species

mammals: 4,300 species

reptiles: 6,000 species

□ 1 LOOK at your writing.

✎ Circle some of your best diagonal swing up joins.

□ 2 Pick the joins that need work. Compare them with the models.
PLAN how to make the joins look more like the models.

□ 3 PRACTICE the joins that need more work.

NOTE: Have you made an improvement in your handwriting? Pick a page of your best handwriting to put in your Student Portfolio.

Cursive Italic Lowercase

JOIN 3: DIAGONAL START BACK

Join 3 is a straight diagonal line from the baseline to the waistline then start back into **o** and **s**.

a/ao diagonal start back

ao | ao co do eo ho io ko lo
Trace & copy. ao

PREFIX: co-

mo no uo zo **co-**cooperate
mo

VOWEL SOUND: O: short O

o copy oxygen
o

VOWEL SOUND: O: long O

o open potato
o

AVOID wave

Photosynthesis (sunlight, carbon dioxide, oxygen, water)

✏️ Circle one of your best diagonal joins into **o**.

a/as diagonal start back

as | as cs ds es hs is ks ls
as

Silent s

ms ns us zs s islands
ms

CONSONANT SOUNDS:
S: regular
S: Z sound

s us this   s is has does
s

PREFIX: dis-, mis-

dis-disability mis-misuse
dis

OPTION: Join 8 shows another way to join into s.

✏️ Circle one of your best diagonal joins into **s**.

PRACTICE here and on lined paper.

26 © 1994 Getty/Dubay

Cursive Italic Lowercase

REVIEW: JOIN 3

JOIN 3 joins are underlined.

Green plants use sunlight, water, and carbon dioxide to make their own food.

As a byproduct, they release oxygen (which we breathe.)

This process is called photo-synthesis.

1. LOOK
2. PLAN
3. PRACTICE

✎ Are you joining into **o** and **s** with a straight diagonal line? Yes___ No___

Zamia   *Dictyota*   *Pteridium*   *Chara*

Cursive Italic Lowercase

JOIN 4: DIAGONAL INTO e

Join 4 is a straight diagonal line to the branching line into the center of e.

a⟶ ae
diagonal
into e

ae ae ce de ee he ie ke le
Trace & copy. ae

VOWEL SOUND:
E: silent

me ne ue ze · e home people
me

VOWEL SOUND:
EE: long E
PHONOGRAMS: -ee, -eed

ee eel keep -ee see -eed seed
ee

PHONOGRAMS:

-eek seek -eel heel -eem seem
eek

NOTE:
Join into e at the branching line.

-een seen -eep keep -eer deer

imaginary branching line ....een

AVOID
ae
↑
scoop

-eet meet -ief chief -ike like
eet

REMINDER: Option:
You may join into m, n, and r using Join 2.

OPTIONAL JOIN
-ite mite en seem seen deer
ite

SUFFIX: -ment

-ment environment fragment
ment

✏ Circle one of your best diagonal joins into e.

NOTE:
E is our most used letter. Take care joining into e.

PRACTICE here and on lined paper.

NOTE: For two-stroke e see INSTRUCTION MANUAL

A source of lead is the mineral galena.

'Lead' in pencils is actually graphite; one of the world's softest minerals.

Cursive Italic Lowercase

REVIEW: JOIN 4

JOIN 4 joins are underlined.

Mi<u>ne</u>rals are natural objects ma<u>de</u> of inorganic matter.

M

REMINDER: Relax your hand. Tap your index finger on the pencil three times to help avoid pinching.

✏️ Are you joining into **e** at the branching line? Yes___ No___

Mi<u>ne</u>rals join to ma<u>ke</u> rocks. Rocks are for<u>me</u>d in th<u>re</u>e ways: by wind and water, by volcanoes, and by pressure.

1. Sedimentary rocks: limestone, sandstone, shale

2. Igneous rocks: basalt, gabro, granite, obsidian

3. Metamorphic rocks: marble, quartzite, schist, slate

M

REMINDER: Tap your index finger on the pencil three times to help avoid pinching. See Pencil Hold on page vi.

1. LOOK at your writing.

2. Pick the joins that need work. Compare them with the models. PLAN how to make the joins look more like the models.

✏️ Circle one of your best diagonal joins into **e**.

3. PRACTICE here and on lined paper.

© 1994 Getty/Dubay

Cursive Italic Lowercase
JOIN 5: HORIZONTAL

Join 5 is a horizontal join at the waistline. Join out of *o, t, f, v, w,* and *x* into every letter except *f*.

o⃗ o⃗n
horizontal
into soft angle

on on om or ox com- combine
Trace & copy. *on*

PREFIXES: com-, con-, mono-

con- connect mono- monorail
con

SUFFIXES: -ion, -or

-ion champion -or author
ion

VOWEL SOUND:
OR: OR sound
SUFFIX: -dom

or orbit order -dom wisdom
or

ou oy oi oj op ov ow
ou

horizontal
into sharp angle

VOWEL SOUNDS:
OU: OU diphthong
OY: OI diphthong
OI: OI diphthong

ou mountain oy boy oi oil
ou

VOWEL SOUNDS:
OW: long O
OW: OU diphthong

ow grow ow flower
ow

DICOT FLOWER
sepals and petals in groups of fours or fives — sedum, dogwood

SUFFIX: -ous

-ous famous
ous

MONOCOT FLOWER
sepals and petals in groups of three or multiples of three — lily

SUFFIX: -ious

-ious delicious ambitious
ious

✎ Circle one of your best joins out of *o*.

PRACTICE here and on lined paper.

Cursive Italic Lowercase - Join 5

→o oo oa
horizontal start back

1. oo oa oc od og oq os
2. oo

VOWEL SOUNDS:
OO: short OO
OO: long OO

3. oo good book oo cool smooth
4. oo

VOWEL SOUND:
OA: long O
PHONOGRAMS: -oat, -oak, -oan

5. oa oak boat -oat -oak -oan
6. oa

→o ot ol
horizontal swing up

7. ot ol oh ob ok -ology biology
8. ot

SUFFIX: -ology
PHONOGRAMS: Write words using these phonograms.

9. -ob -ock -od -og -oke -old
10.
11. -one -ong -oo -ood -ook -ool
12.
13. -oom -oon -oop -oot -op
14.
15. -ope -ore -orn -ot -ow (ō) -ow (ou)
16.

NOTE: This diagonal join is different from the join above.

→o oe
diagonal into e

✎ Are you joining out of o with a horizontal line?   Yes___ No___

17. oe doe foe hoe roe toe woe
18. oe

NOTE: Join out of o into e with a diagonal line from the waistline. The counter of e is smaller.

✎ Circle your best diagonal join into e.

PRACTICE the joins that need more work.

19.
20.

NOTE:
See THE NEW READING TEACHER'S BOOK OF LISTS, Phonograms, pages 124-133.

Cursive Italic Lowercase - Join 5

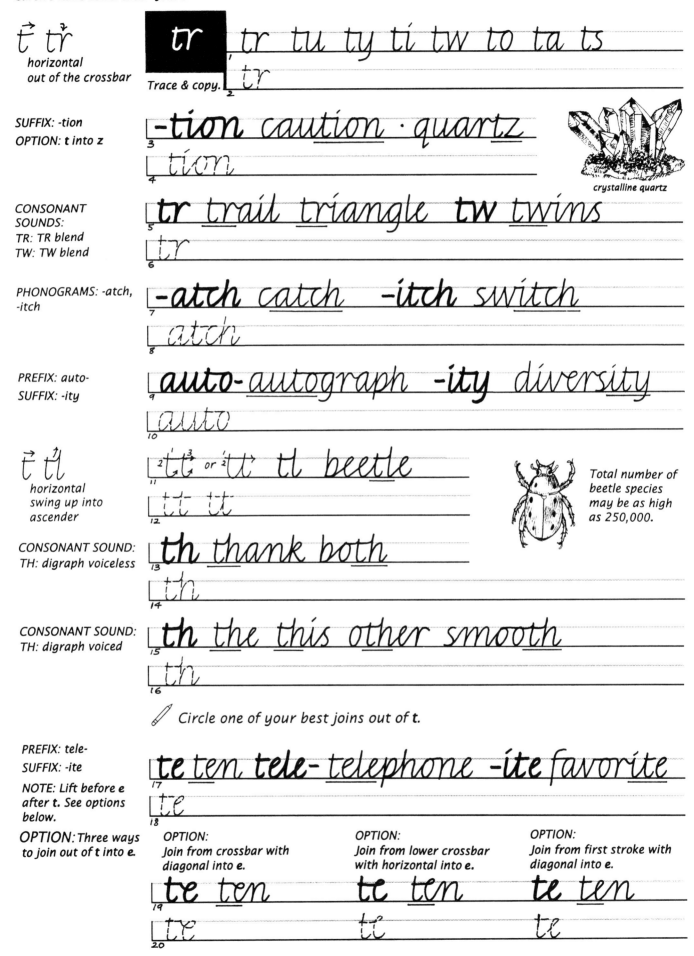

Cursive Italic Lowercase - Join 5

horizontal out of the crossbar

Trace & copy.

fr fu fy fi fo fa fs

CONSONANT SOUND:
FR: FR blend
SUFFIX: -ify

fr fresh fruit -ify identify

CONSONANT SOUND:
FL: FL blend

fl fly   flea   flew

NOTE: Join f and t with one crossbar.

PHONOGRAMS: -aft, -ift

ft ft -aft craft -ift lift

✏ Circle one of your best joins out of **f**.

NOTE: Lift before e after t. See options.

fe fe life

OPTION: Join with diagonal out of crossbar of f.
fe fe life

OPTION: Join from lower crossbar of f into e.
fe fe life

Copy this paragraph on lined paper. First place paper over this paragraph and trace, then copy.

"Every part of this earth is sacred to my people. Every shining pine needle, every sandy shore, every mist in the dark woods, every clearing, and every humming insect is holy in the memory and experience of my people. ...All things are connected.

— Chief Seattle

Excerpts from a letter to President Pierce written in 1855 and attributed to Chief Seattle, Duwamish tribe, state of Washington.

Cursive Italic Lowercase - Join 5

v⃗ vn horizontal

vn | vn vu vy vi vo va vs vt
Trace & copy. vn

v⃗ ve diagonal into e

PHONOGRAMS: -ave, -ive, -ove

SUFFIXES: -ive, -ves

ve -ave save -ive live -ove love
ve

-ive active -ves calves hooves
ive

w⃗ wn horizontal

wn | wn wr wu wy wo wa ws
wn

CONSONANT SOUND: WR: R sound

PHONOGRAMS: -awn, -own

wr write -awn dawn -own town
wr

PHONOGRAM: -owl

wt wl wh wk -owl howl
wt

CONSONANT SOUND: WH: digraph (HW blend)

PHONOGRAM: -awk

wh whale -awk hawk
wh

w⃗ we diagonal into e

we web well wet
we

Zone-tailed hawk

✏ Circle one of your best joins out of **v** and out of **w**.

x⃗ xu horizontal

xu | xu xy xi xo xa xt xl xe

x⃗ xe diagonal into e

✏ Circle one of your best joins out of **x**.

PRACTICE here and on lined paper.

34 © 1994 Getty/Dubay

Cursive Italic Lowercase

REVIEW: JOIN 5

JOIN 5 joins are underlined.

> The earth is divided into seven continents: Africa, Antarctica, Asia, Australia, Europe, North America, and South America.

1 LOOK at your writing.
CHECKLIST
___ letter shape
___ letter size
___ letter slope
___ letter spacing

2 PLAN how to make the joins look more like the models.

✎ Circle some of your best joins out of **o**, **t**, **f**, and **v**.

Copy this paragraph on lined paper. First place paper over this paragraph and trace, then copy.

3 PRACTICE on lined paper.

NOTE:
In this paragraph, the join into n, m, r, and x is Join 2, shown on page 24.

> There are nine major biomes or vegetation zones: chaparral, deciduous forest, desert, evergreen forest (taiga), grassland/savanna, mountain, polar ice, tropical forest, and tundra.

✎ Circle some of your best horizontal joins.

35

© 1994 Getty/Dubay

Cursive Italic Lowercase

JOIN 6: DIAGONAL OUT OF *r*

Join 6 is a short diagonal line out of *r* into all letters except *f*.

r diagonal

rn rn rm rr ru ry ri rp ro
Trace & copy.

PHONOGRAMS: -arm, -orn, -urn

ra rc rd rs -arm alarm

NOTE: Bend arm of *r* at the waistline before joining.
AVOID *rn* looking like *m*

-orn horn -urn Saturn

Saturn's rings of whirling ice.

SUFFIXES: -ary, -arium

-ary library -arium aquarium

PHONOGRAMS: -ard, -arp, -arn

-ard card -arp harp -arn barn

PHONOGRAMS: -art, -irt, -ort, -url, -ark, -ork.

rt rl rh rb rk re -art smart

-irt shirt -ort sport -url curl

Double r

-ark mark -ork fork rr error

PREFIX: re-
PHONOGRAMS: -are, -ore

re rewrite -are care -ore more

✏ Circle one of your best joins out of *r*.

PRACTICE here and on lined paper.

36 © 1994 Getty/Dubay

Cursive Italic Lowercase

SUFFIXES: -ward, -ern, -ry, -ery

-ward forward -ern western
ward

-ry poetry -ery pottery
ry

REVIEW: JOIN 6

JOIN 6 joins are underlined.

There are eight planets in our solar system. In order of their closeness to the sun, they are: Mercury, Venus, Earth, Mars, Jupiter, Saturn, Uranus, & Neptune.*

REMINDER: Optional join into e out of t.

NOTE: E and T combine to form the ampersand.

&T &

'Et' is the latin word for 'and'.

* Pluto is now considered a dwarf planet according to the International Astronomical Union, August 2006.

1. LOOK at your writing. ✏ Are you joining out of **r** with a short diagonal line?   Yes___ No___

2. PLAN which letters need work. Compare them with the models.

3. PRACTICE on lined paper.

NOTE: The join out of **r** needs more practice than any other join. Legibility depends on it being done well.

The planet Earth is ninety-three million miles from the sun.

Neptune
Uranus
Saturn
Jupiter
Mars
Earth
Venus
Mercury
sun

© 1994 Getty/Dubay

Cursive Italic Lowercase

JOIN 7: HORIZONTAL TO DIAGONAL

Join 7 is a horizontal line at the baseline blending into a diagonal line. Follow back out of **s**, **b**, and **p** and join into all letters except **f** and **z**.

s sn
horizontal to diagonal

Trace & copy. sn sn sm su sy si sp sw so
sn

se st sl sh sk ss or ss
se

CONSONANT SOUNDS:
SN: SN blend
SM: SM blend

sn snow snail sm smile smart
sn

SP: SP blend
SW: SW blend

sp space respond sw swim swirl
sp

ST: ST blend
SL: SL blend

st story best sl slope slant
st

SH: digraph
SK: SK blend

sh shape finish sk sky task
sh

SUFFIXES: -less, -est, -ist, -ship, -ism, -ness

-less homeless -est smallest
-less

-ist artist -ship friendship
-ist

-ism heroism -ness happiness
-ism

✎ Circle one of your best joins out of **s**.

PRACTICE here and on lined paper.

Cursive Italic Lowercase - Join 7

b bn
horizontal to diagonal

CONSONANT SOUNDS:
BR: BR blend
BL: BL blend
Double **b**

br Trace & copy.   br bu by bi bl bb bo be
br

br library   bl blend   bb bubble
br

p pn
horizontal to diagonal

CONSONANT SOUNDS:
PR: PR blend
PL: PL blend
PH: F sound
PREFIX: pro-
Double **p**

pr   pr pu py pi pl pp po pe
pr

pr practice improve **pl** please
pr

ph photo **pro-**protect **pp** apple
ph

✏️ Circle one of your best joins out of **b** and out of **p**.

REVIEW: JOIN 7

JOIN 7 joins are underlined.

Our solar system consists of one star (which we call the sun,) eight planets, over thirty thousand asteroids, and countless comets.

1. LOOK
CHECKLIST
___ letter shape
___ letter size
___ letter slope
___ letter spacing

2. PLAN

3. PRACTICE

✏️ Are you following back out of **b**, **p**, and **s** into a diagonal? Yes___ No___

Cursive Italic Lowercase

JOIN 8: DIAGONAL TO HORIZONTAL

Join 8 is a diagonal line from the baseline blending into a horizontal line at the waistline. Join into a, c, d, g, q, and s.

a↗ aa↗
diagonal
to horizontal

aa aa ca da ea ha ia ka la
Trace & copy. aa

ma na ua za sa ba pa
ma

VOWEL SOUNDS:
EA: long E
EA: short E sound

ea east neat sea ea weather
ea

PHONOGRAMS: Write
a word using each
phonogram.

-eak -eal -eam -ear -eat

Silent c

-ace -ack -ice c science

SUFFIX: -ian

-ian musician mathematician
ian

✏ Circle one of your best joins into **a**.

a↗ ac↗
diagonal
to horizontal

Double c
ac ac ec ic uc sc cc accept
ac

CONSONANT SOUND:
SC: SC blend

sc school telescope describe
sc

✏ Circle one of your best joins into **c**.

PRACTICE here and
on lined paper.

Cursive Italic Lowercase - Join 8

a͢d a͢d
diagonal
to horizontal

Double d
ad | ad ed id ud **dd** addition
Trace & copy. ad

PHONOGRAMS: Write a word using each phonogram.
-ad -ade -ed -eed -id -ide

SUFFIX: -ed
-and -end -ind -ed challenged

✏ Circle one of your best joins into **d**.

a͢g a͢q
diagonal
to horizontal

ag aq | ag eg ig ug aq eq iq
ag

CONSONANT SOUND: NG: NG
ng sing length -ang -ing
ng

PHONOGRAMS: Write a word using each phonogram.
-ung -ag -ig -ug -eg

CONSONANT SOUND: Q: KW sound
qu quiet equal qu

✏ Circle your best join into **g** and into **q**.

NOTE: You may join out of a few capitals such as **C, K,** and **R.**

Comets follow
an immense
orbit around
the sun.

This is part of the 200 ft. long Bayeux tapestry.

Halley's comet appeared in 1066 as recorded in the Bayeux tapestry embroidered in the 11th century. This comet has been recorded since 240 B.C. and appears every 75 to 76 years. It last appeared in 1986.

Cursive Italic Lowercase - Join 8

a/ as diagonal to horizontal

as | as es is us **Double s** ss success

Trace & copy. as

PHONOGRAMS: Write a word using each phonogram.

-ase -ash -ask -ast -est -ise

NOTE: AVOID wave *is*

-ish -isk -us -ush -ust

REVIEW: JOIN 8

JOIN 8 joins are underlined.

Galaxy: a large group of stars isolated in space from other such groups. Our galaxy is the Milky Way, containing at least one billion stars. One of these stars is our sun.

REMINDER: Optional join out of **t** into **e**.

REMINDER: Keep capitals, ascenders and descenders their correct size to avoid tangling.

[1] LOOK at your writing.

[2] Pick the joins that need work. Compare them with the models. PLAN how to make the joins look more like the models.

[3] PRACTICE: Have you made an improvement in your handwriting? Pick a page of your best handwriting to put in your Student Portfolio.

✏ Circle some of your best diagonal to horizontal joins.

Shapes of galaxies: Ellipticals, Spirals (Milky Way), Barred spirals, and Irregulars. (left to right)

Cursive Italic Lowercase

LIFTS: Lift before **f** and **z**; lift after **g**, **j**, **q**, and **y**.

Joins are natural spacers. When letters are not joined, place letters close together. AVOID gap.

af az   af az ef ez if iz of oz
af

Double f
Double z

ff off zz pizza ff

ga ju qu yu   ga ju qu yu
ga

CONSONANT SOUNDS:
GH: silent
GL: GL blend

gh light neighbor gl globe glass
gh

GR: GR blend
Double g

gr agree gravity gg juggle
gr

CONSONANT SOUNDS:
G: regular
G: J sound
J: regular
Q: KW sound
Y: consonant
Y: long E
Y: long I

g go g gym j join q quiet y you
g

y everyone y myself e

✏ When lifting are you keeping letters close together to AVOID gaps?

REMINDER:
Keep letters close together when lifting between letters.

Beyond our galaxy in all directions hang countless other galaxies. More than a billion galaxies are visible through telescopes. B

PRACTICE even letter spacing.

waistline →

BASELINE ONLY: Write on the baseline and imagine where the waistline is. (It is halfway between the baselines.) This is like writing on wide-ruled notebook paper.

43   © 1994 Getty/Dubay

Cursive Italic

SIZE: 4mm bodyheight; 6mm capital and ascender height and descender length

body height 4mm — *A quick brown fox jumps over the lazy dog.*

OPTIONAL JOIN

br um er

✏ Are your letters the correct height?

5° SLOPE:

Write your signature using cursive italic. Write names of your family: mother, father, sisters, brothers, grandparents, aunts or uncles.

✏ Are your downstrokes parallel to the slope lines? Yes___ No___

SPACING: Use even spacing in words. Joins are natural spacers. When letters are not joined, place letters close together.

Write your signature using cursive italic.

✏ Are you spacing the letters evenly? Yes___ No___

CHECKLIST
___ letter shape
___ letter size
___ letter slope
___ letter spacing

BASELINE ONLY: Write on the baseline and imagine where the waistline is. (It is halfway between the baselines.)

AVOID tangling capitals, ascenders, and descenders.

✏ How is your handwriting getting better?

44

© 1994 Getty/Dubay

Slope; Speed

SLOPE GUIDELINES:

A 5° letter slope is used for basic and cursive.

OPTIONS: You have a choice of slope--from a vertical of 0° to a slope of 15°. This is the choice range:

Which is your most comfortable letter slope? Whichever letter slope you choose, use that slope for all your writing.

LOOK at your writing.

✎ Do you have an even letter slope?
                      Yes___ No___

SLOPE GUIDE:

Make your own slope guide to fit your choice of letter slope. Place a sheet of notebook paper at an angle under your writing paper and line up the lines with your letter slope.

✎ Do your letters have different slopes?
                      Yes___ No___

PLAN how to write with an even letter slope. Use the following exercise to find a comfortable slope for you.

1. write word

2. draw slope lines over letters

3. pick one slope

4. draw parallel lines

5. write over slope lines

Choose a letter slope and write all your letters using that slope.

Use paper clips or removable tape to hold the two sheets together. On the undersheet outline the edge of the writing paper so you know where to place the next sheet of paper.

   0°   5°   10°   15°

SPEED: TIMED WRITING
Use the timed writing to help increase speed. The goal is to increase the number of words written per minute. Begin by writing the following sentence (or another sentence) as a warm-up.

A quick brown fox jumps over the lazy dog.

1. TIME LENGTH: 1 MINUTE Write the sentence at your most comfortable speed. If you finish before the time is up, begin the sentence again. Count the number of words written. Write this number in the margin.

2. TIME LENGTH: 1 MINUTE Write the sentence a little faster. Try to add one or two more words to your total. Count the number of words written.

3. TIME LENGTH: 1 MINUTE Write the sentence as fast as you can. Count the number of words written.

4. TIME LENGTH: 1 MINUTE Write the sentence at a comfortable speed. Count the number of words written. Write the number in the margin.

Repeat process once a month.

✎ Compare the total of # 4 to # 1.
   Did you increase the number of words written by one or more? Yes___ No___

EYES CLOSED
Using the same sentence, do this exercise as a follow-up to the timed writing. Use a non-lined sheet of paper. Close your eyes. Picture in your mind's eye the shape of each letter as you write. Take all the time you need. You may be amazed how well you can write with your eyes closed.

© 1994 Getty/Dubay

CURSIVE ITALIC CAPITALS

	EGYPTIAN HIEROGLYPH	PHOENICIAN LETTER	GREEK LETTER	ROMAN LETTER	BASIC ITALIC	CURSIVE ITALIC CAPITAL

A — 5° slope
1st stroke: curve exit serif
3rd stroke: extended entrance of crossbar

Ox

Ghana — *Accra* India — *Agra* Turkey — *Ankara* Georgia — *Atlanta*

other cities beginning with A

B — 2nd stroke: curve entrance serif

House

Thailand — *Bangkok* Lebanon — *Beirut* India — *Bombay* Massachusetts — *Boston*

other cities beginning with B

C — no change

Camel

India — *Calcutta* Columbia — *Cali* Venezuela — *Caracas* Illinois — *Chicago*

other cities beginning with C

D — 2nd stroke: curve entrance serif

Door

India — *Delhi* Colorado — *Denver* Indonesia — *Djakarta* Ireland — *Dublin*

other cities beginning with D

1. LOOK
2. PLAN
3. PRACTICE

CHECKLIST
___ letter shape
___ letter size
___ letter slope
___ letter spacing

✏ Circle some of your best capitals.

© 1994 Getty/Dubay

Cursive Italic Capitals

	EGYPTIAN HIEROGLYPH	PHOENICIAN LETTER	GREEK LETTER	ROMAN LETTER	BASIC ITALIC	CURSIVE ITALIC CAPITAL

E — 2nd stroke: curve entrance serif

BEHOLD

Edinburgh (Scotland) Edmonton (Canada) El Paso (Texas) Essen (Germany)

other cities beginning with E

F — 2nd stroke: curve entrance serif

HOOK/NAIL

Florence (Italy) Fortaleza (Brazil) Frankfurt (Germany) Fushon (China)

other cities beginning with F

G — changes to one-stroke: curve exit serif

(Added in the 3rd century B.C. The Romans added a bar to C to form G.)

Genoa (Italy) Ghent (Belgium) Glasgow (Scotland) Geneva (Switzerland)

other cities beginning with G

H —
1st stroke: sharp angle entrance serif, curve exit serif
2nd stroke: curve entrance serif begins slightly higher
3rd stroke: extended crossbar

FENCE

Hangchou (China) Helsinki (Finland) Honolulu (Hawaii) Hsian (China)

other cities beginning with H

1. LOOK
2. PLAN
3. PRACTICE

CHECKLIST
___ letter shape
___ letter size
___ letter slope
___ letter spacing

✏️ *Circle some of your best capitals.*

Cursive Italic Capitals

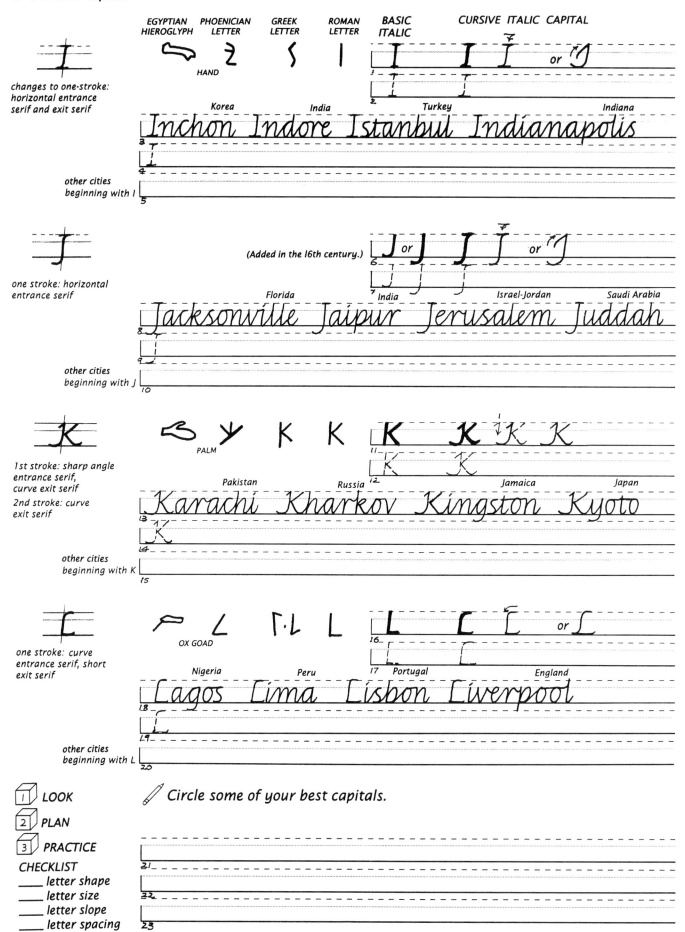

Cursive Italic Capitals

| EGYPTIAN HIEROGLYPH | PHOENICIAN LETTER | GREEK LETTER | ROMAN LETTER | BASIC ITALIC | CURSIVE ITALIC CAPITAL |

M — 1st stroke: curve exit serif

WATER

Madrid (Spain) Manila (Philippines) Memphis (Tennessee) Moscow (Russia)

other cities beginning with M

N — 1st stroke: curve exit serif; 3rd stroke: soft curve entrance serif begins slightly higher

FISH

NOTE: 3rd stroke begins higher

...pur (India) Nairobi (Kenya) Nanking (China) Newark (New Jersey)

other cities beginning with N

O — no changes

EYE

Omaha (Nebraska) Osaka (Japan) Oslo (Norway) Ottawa (Canada)

other cities beginning with O

P — 2nd stroke: curve entrance serif

MOUTH

Paris (France) Pasadena (California) Portland (Oregon) Prague (Czech Republic)

other cities beginning with P

[1] LOOK
[2] PLAN
[3] PRACTICE
CHECKLIST
___ letter shape
___ letter size
___ letter slope
___ letter spacing

✏ Circle some of your best capitals.

Cursive Italic Capitals

| EGYPTIAN HIEROGLYPH | PHOENICIAN LETTER | GREEK LETTER | ROMAN LETTER | BASIC ITALIC | CURSIVE ITALIC CAPITAL |

Q — 2nd stroke: short exit serif
KNOT

Quebec (Canada) Quezon City (Philippines) Quito (Ecuador) Quincy (Massachusetts)

other cities beginning with Q

R — 2nd stroke: curve entrance serif; 3rd stroke: soft curve exit serif
HEAD

Rabat (Morocco) Recife (Brazil) Rochester (New York) Rome (Italy)

other cities beginning with R

S — no changes
TOOTH

Sapporo (Japan) Seattle (Washington) Suez (Egypt) Sydney (Australia)

other cities beginning with S

T — 2nd stroke: curve entrance serif
MARK/SIGN

Tokyo (Japan) Toledo (Ohio) Toronto (Canada) Turin (Italy)

other cities beginning with T

1. LOOK
2. PLAN
3. PRACTICE

CHECKLIST
___ letter shape
___ letter size
___ letter slope
___ letter spacing

✏ Circle some of your best capitals.

© 1994 Getty/Dubay

Cursive Italic Capitals

| EGYPTIAN HIEROGLYPH | PHOENICIAN LETTER | GREEK LETTER | ROMAN LETTER | BASIC ITALIC | CURSIVE ITALIC CAPITAL |

U
one-stroke: soft angle entrance serif

(Added in the 16th century.) U U U

Russia — Ufa Mongolia — Ulan Bator New York — Utica The Netherlands — Utrecht

other cities beginning with U

V
one-stroke: curve entrance serif

Y F V V V V
HOOK/NAIL

Chile — Valparaiso Canada — Vancouver Italy — Venice Austria — Vienna

other cities beginning with V

W
one-stroke: curve entrance serif

(Added in the 11th century.) W W W

Poland — Warsaw District of Columbia — Washington Canada — Winnipeg

other cities beginning with W

X
1st stroke: curve entrance serif and exit serif

⩻ X X X X X
PROP

Greece — Xanthi Ohio — Xenia Mexico — Xilitla Mexico — Xochimilco

other cities beginning with X

1. LOOK
2. PLAN
3. PRACTICE

✏️ Circle some of your best capitals.

CHECKLIST
___ letter shape
___ letter size
___ letter slope
___ letter spacing

Cursive Italic Capitals

□1 LOOK
□2 PLAN
□3 PRACTICE
CHECKLIST
___ shape
___ size
___ slope
___ spacing

✏ Circle some of your best capitals.

✏ How is your handwriting getting better?

TIMELINE

Egyptian	Phoenician	Early Greek	Classical Greek	Roman				
3000	2500	2000	1500	1000	500 B.C.	0	500 A.D.	1000	1500	2000

Italic

NOTE:
For basic & cursive capital assessment questions see INSTRUCTION MANUAL.

CONGRATULATIONS! You have completed this book. You are improving your handwriting day by day. Good Work!

As you write on your own, continue to practice good handwriting habits: even slope, even size, and even spacing. Hooray for you and your good handwriting!

✏ Turn to page viii and write your Post-test. Use your best cursive italic handwriting.

© 1994 Getty/DUBAY

SPECIAL ASSIGNMENT: WRITE A LETTER/BOOKLET

Write a letter to a relative, a friend, or a pen-pal.

ROUGH DRAFT: Compose your letter in pencil. Use lined paper or 4mm lines on page 56.

CHECK WORDING: Edit for capitals, spelling and punctuation.

BOOKLET: Make the surprise booklet.
Materials: sheet of light or medium weight paper and scissors.
A 28 cm x 43 cm (11" x 17") sheet will give a finished size of 10.8 cm x 14 cm (4 1/4" x 5 1/2"). This size will fit an A-2 envelope.

NOTE: In illustrations dotted line indicates fold that occurs within the given step. Solid lines within rectangle indicate folds previously established.

1. Fold AB to CD to establish EF.
2. Open back to original size.
3. Fold AC to BD to establish GH.
4. Fold GH to AC/BD to establish IJ.
5. Open to previous fold (GH/AB/CD).
6. With scissors, cut KL by cutting halfway between GH, stopping at fold IJ.
7. Open to original size ABCD.
8. Refold AB to CD as in #1.
9. Grasp E/AC with left hand and F/BD with right hand, then push hands together, establishing 3 pages on one side and 1 on the other.
10. Fold remaining leaf over the other three pages. Two leaves have folds at the top and two on the fore edge of the booklet.

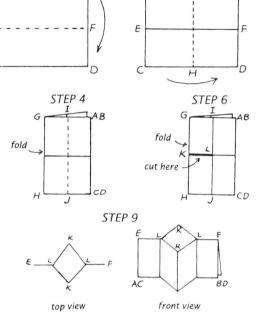

STEP 10

completed booklet

beginning of letter

middle of letter

end of letter

Arrange letters on the three two-page spreads of the letter/card. Leave a one inch margin on all sides. Decorate the cover with a design, perhaps using the name of the person the letter is for.

FINAL COPY: Use your best handwriting for your final copy. Take your time.
Write your final copy with a pencil or pen.

ENVELOPE: Address the envelope using your best handwriting.
On the first line write the name of the person you are writing to.
On the second line write the person's house number and street name (apartment number, Post Office Box number, etc.).
On the third line write the city, state, and zip code. (Add country if needed.)

NOTE: For an envelope template see INSTRUCTION MANUAL.

Take an envelope apart.
Spread it out and place on a larger piece of paper.

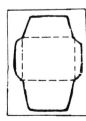
Trace around the edge. Cut out the new envelope. Fold envelope. Glue or tape to hold together.

glue or tape

In the upper left hand corner write your return address.

© 1994 Getty/Dubay

READING LOOPED CURSIVE
Comparing Cursive Italic with Looped Cursive
NOTE: letter shape, letter slope, and size of capitals, ascenders, and descenders

Look at the examples of cursive italic and looped cursive. Compare the two styles of writing. Notice the differences in letter shape, letter slope, capital height, ascender height, and descender length.

There are many styles of writing you need to be able to read. Practice reading looped cursive. To help read the looped cursive letters, each name contains both a capital letter and its lowercase version.

SHAPE:
Look at the different shapes of the looped cursive lowercase letters **b, f, r, s,** and **z** and the capital letters **F, G, I, J, Q, S, T, V, X,** and **Z**.

SLOPE:
Look at the slope difference. Cursive Italic letter slope is 5° and looped cursive is 30°.

SIZE:
Look at the size difference. Cursive italic capitals, ascenders, and descenders are 1 1/2 body heights. Looped cursive capitals, ascenders and descenders are 2 body heights.

Compare the absence of loops in cursive italic with the many loops in looped cursive. Look at how the capitals, ascenders, and descenders become tangled in the looped cursive.
Loop-free italic is easier to read.

CURSIVE ITALIC 5° slope	LOOPED CURSIVE 30° slope
Angela	Angela
Barbara	Barbara
Cecilia	Cecilia
David	David
Eugene	Eugene
Fifi	Fifi
Gregory	Gregory
Hannah	Hannah
Irving	Irving
Jojo	Jojo
Kirk	Kirk
Lillian	Lillian
Malcolm	Malcolm
Nancy	Nancy
Otto	Otto
Philippa	Philippa
Quequeg	Quequeg
Richard	Richard
Susan	Susan
Trent	Trent
Ursula	Ursula
Vivian	Vivian
Woodrow	Woodrow
Xerxes	Xerxes
Yonny	Yonny
Zanzi	Zanzi

© 1994 Getty/Dubay

5mm lines

4mm lines